P9-DMP-570

Broadcast Basics

429392

070.4
Cap

429392

Broadcast Basics

A Beginner's Guide to Television News Reporting and Production

Yvonne Cappé

Marion Street Press, Inc.
Oak Park, Illinois

SHELBYVILLE-SHELBY COUNTY
PUBLIC LIBRARY

Copyright © 2006 Yvonne Cappé

All Rights Reserved

ISBN 1-933338-14-8
Printed in U.S.A.
Printing 10 9 8 7 6 5 4 3 2 1

Marion Street Press, Inc.
PO Box 2249
Oak Park, IL 60303
866-443-7987
www.marionstreetpress.com

Dedicated to Roger and Jaime — the lights of my life.
You've always been there.

Contents

Acknowledgments

This book is a compilation of comments, materials and experiences gathered during more than 20 years in the broadcast industry and also relies on other source materials. Original sources and references are cited as accurately as possible and/or covered by fair use provisions of the Copyright Act.

Special thanks go to the following: John Spain, John Camp, Bill Payer, Bob Papper, Jerry Gumbert, Mackie Morris, Boyd Hubbert, Investigative Reporters and Editors, Society of Professional Journalists, Radio-TV News Directors Association, and National Press Photographers Association.

About the Author

Yvonne Cappé is a broadcast journalism professor at the University of Kentucky and a former newsroom executive producer. She is the recipient of the Excellence in Teaching Award from the College of Communications and Information Studies at the University of Kentucky.

Preface

So You Want to be a Journalist

News *n.pl.* **1.** New information; information previously unknown. **2.** *a)* recent happenings *b)* reports of these. **3.** A newscast — make news, to do something reported as news.

- Webster's New World Dictionary

Journalism *n.* **1.** *a)* **the** collection and editing of news for presentation through the media *b)* the public press *c)* an academic study concerned with the collection and editing of news or the management of a news medium.

Journalist *n.* **1.** *a)* a person engaged in journalism; especially: a writer or editor for a news medium *b)* a writer who aims at a mass audience.
-Merriam-Webster's Collegiate Dictionary

When you read the above definitions do you recognize yourself? I hope you do!

Journalism has been described alternately as a skill, a craft, a calling. I prefer to think of it as all three.

I want you to take away from this text a set of journalistic skills. You should be able to develop information, to source it out, to visually present that information through your use of sophisticated electronic equipment.

You should use those journalistic skills to produce a news product — a piece of journalism. I want you to take the technical and writing skills to create information readily understandable by a viewing or listening public.

More importantly, I want you to be guided to this calling by a strong inner impulse coupled with a conviction to present the truth, unbiased by agendas set by others or even yourself.

Journalism should not be taken lightly

Here are a few things journalism is not:

■ A way to get your face on TV
■ A way to apply pressure for personal gain
■ The assumption of information as fact
■ A distortion of the truth by manipulation of words, pictures, or information

Journalism is:

■ Freedom of speech
■ A vehicle for social change

■ A public trust
■ A forum for political and social accountability

Not every society has the journalistic freedoms granted by the Constitution of the United States. The First Amendment to the Constitution states:

"***Congress shall make no law*** respecting an establishment of religion, or prohibiting the free exercise there of; or ***abridging the freedom of speech, or of the press***; or the right of the people to peaceably to assemble, and to petition the government for a redress of grievances."

The work you do as a reporter is a sacred trust. Your reports should reflect your efforts to examine the facts thoroughly, to present the story fairly, and to stand confidently behind your work. What you say and do will be held up to public scrutiny. If your fact-finding has been shoddy, your sources questionable, and your reporting incomplete, YOU will be held accountable. Not only will your bosses hold you accountable (you just embarrassed them in front of thousands of viewers and left them open to lawsuits) but your credibility with the public, with community leaders, even your friends, will be held in question.

As a reporter, the only thing you begin and end each day with is your ***credibility***. The public has a very long memory. If you lose your credibility, chances are it will haunt you throughout your career. The news business is a very tight community that feeds on the gossip and missteps of its members. Someone in the business will always know someone else in the next market that would love to know the dirt.

Chapter 1

Writing for Broadcast

Fasten your seatbelts! I'm going to tell you something that will "stop the presses."

You will now unlearn all the rules of writing every English teacher has taught you since the third grade! In fact, the simplistic writing of the first and second grade (See Jane run. Run, Jane, run.) is now your goal.

Writing for broadcast requires clear, concise, and cliché-free structure. It is as simple as Subject-Verb-Object. Your story will have a greater effect if you keep this in mind: **one subject per sentence; one theme per story.**

Why so simple? Think about it. Broadcast transforms your words into electronic impulses that are there one moment, then gone. When you read the newspaper, a magazine, or a textbook, you can back up and re-read that complex sentence with multiple clauses, break it down, and then comprehend the context. Unlike the previous sentence, you can't back up the spoken word.

Another important characteristic of broadcast writing is the conversational tone. Often an insecure reporter will try to overcompensate and used lofty words, phrases, and sentence structure in hopes of convincing the viewer that the reporter is intelligent! But in reality all this does is make the viewer work harder to comprehend and in doing so, the viewer risks losing track of the continual stream of information. When you're speaking with your parents or your best friend, do you use such complicated language? No. So why would you make it harder than necessary for someone who doesn't know you at all?

As a broadcast reporter you will need to take each story and figure out what is the most important fact. You should ask yourself before you begin any story, "**WHY** do I care?" This is where you begin to develop your news judgment. If you cannot answer the "**WHY**" question, then perhaps you need to dig deeper or find another story. Remember reporting has a competitive component. You will find that reporters at competing stations will also have the same story. You must find a way to do it better — better sources, better storytelling, better visuals. Viewers have plenty of choices; you want them to recognize your work as the most accurate, most thorough, and most compelling.

Storytelling

When reporting think of telling a story. Remember the fairy tales of childhood? Sure you do! Why? Because they were simple, they were told in a conversational, one-on-one tone, and they were structured. The storyteller used the structure of beginning, middle, and end. The storyteller painted word pictures to stimulate your imagination. You must do the same with every news story.

Every "good" story (report) has a beginning, middle, and an end. Let's look at Goldilocks and the Three Bears.

Beginning: Once upon a time there were three bears that lived in a little house in the deep woods. Their names were Papa Bear, Momma Bear, and Baby Bear. One lovely, spring day they decided to go for a walk.

Now before you think I've totally lost it, notice I just properly identified the sources (who), their location (where), the time (when), the activity (what), and the reason (why). Your stories must contain the 5-W's of who, what, where, when, and why. Leaving one out will result in an incomplete report. You must also go a step further and include "how."

Middle: While they were gone a little girl with golden locks found their house. Goldilocks went in and found three bowls of porridge on the table. The first bowl was Poppa Bear's and it was too hot. The second bowl was Momma Bear's and it was too cold. But the smallest bowl was Baby Bear's and it was just right, so Goldilocks ate up all the porridge.

Are you getting the picture? Goldilocks goes through the same repetitive action for chairs and beds. Repetition helps us remember — be aware of it in your copy. You don't have to continually use different words with the same meaning to tell a "good" story/report.

End: When Goldilocks saw the three bears she jumped up and ran out of the little house in the deep woods. Goldilocks was never heard from again and the three bears lived happily ever after.

Remember every good story has a beginning, middle, and end; an introduction, a body, a closure. Write conversationally. Paint word pictures. Be creative with your words, not with the facts.

Broadcast Structure

Time is of the essence in broadcast. That is why we write in the active voice and use a simple sentence structure. But there are other challenges before us. Because time is so scarce in broadcast, we want to get to the facts, and in television the pictures, quickly. We must sift through our facts and our interviews to find the reason we care. Remember, you must give the audience a reason to care about a story. It may be that the viewer empathizes with the story. They may have experienced a similar event. It may be shocking either in the sense of brutality or outrage. The story should

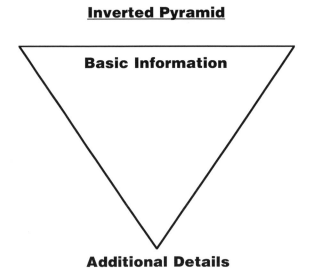

Inverted Pyramid

Basic Information

Additional Details

have an emotional appeal on some level.

In print and most of your English classes you learned to write in the inverted pyramid style. The wide base was at the top narrowing down to information of lesser importance at the bottom. Print writers use this style because copy editors were more likely to cut information from a story at the end to make it fit their size requirements.

For broadcast we write in more of a diamond pattern. We begin with an introduction; fill in the facts, and then close. Beginning, middle, and end. Remember?

You will find this pattern repeated over and over in the

Diamond Pattern

Beginning/Introduction

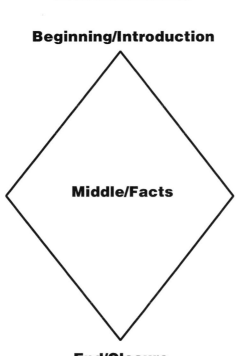

Middle/Facts

End/Closure

Dates

"Today" is a throw away word. Often "today" is used to end a sentence simply because the writer can think of no other way! Worse, what happens when the overnight producer decides to use your 11 p.m. story in the next morning's newscast? Unless referencing a date in the past or in the future, leave dates out of the body of your story, which allows for their use in your story lead in.

stories and their formats. To get to the beginning, you must use your news judgment (critical thinking) to determine the lead. The lead is what is "new" about the story. What is the most important fact? You must also determine if story is newsworthy. How do you decide that? What is the first most important fact? The second? Where does the story occur? Is it in your market/broadcast area? Is it timely? Who will be affected? How prominent are the players? Is there a conflict/opposing side of the issue? Is the story about an average person doing unusual things or an unusual person doing everyday activities? These are just a few of the questions you should ask in addition to "Why do I care?"

Active v. Passive Voice

Another characteristic of broadcast writing is the use of active voice rather than passive voice. Do not confuse voice with tense: Voice indicates direction of a verb's action. Tense deals with the time of a verb.

Because of the time limitation placed on a story, the "weight" of each word must be crafted carefully. That is why writing in the active voice is so important.

Advantages of the Active Voice

■ Straight-line meaning. The listener can understand the copy better because it flows in a straight line. Subject-verb-object.

■ Tighter copy, fewer words. The more time you eliminate by using active voice rather than passive voice, the more time to better tell your story. This is especially important when a producer tells you there is only a 1:15 for your package.

■ Complete reporting. The passive voice tempts you to leave out information, such as the identity of the verb's actor.

■ More interesting copy. Passive voice causes you to write the same old things the same old ways. By using active voice you select active verbs, and you achieve a fresher more interesting style. You paint word pictures.

Ages

Viewers do not care about ages unless the person is very old or very young.

Example: "The 80-year-old woman was mugged."

Example: "The 10-month-old child was found crawling around the parking lot."

No one cares about the ages of a 35-year-old woman who was mugged or a 42-year-old man whose car struck a tree. The age should be used only when it evokes an emotion in the story.

Remember, a sentence is active voice if the receiver (object) of the verb's action follows the verb. The subject-verb-object structure almost guarantees active voice. Let's analyze these passive voice sentences.

The car was stolen by the man.
The horse was raced along the fence.
The player was heard across the football field.
The crowd's attention was focused on the rescuer.

Each sentence has a verb phrase. Each verb phrase contains a form of the "to be" verb. In each sentence the receiver of the action comes before the verb.

Passive Voice Solutions

So how do you resolve your passive voice problem? Try these solutions.

■ Relocate the actor and turn the sentence around.
The man stole the car.

■ Identify and insert the missing actor.
The jockey raced the horse along the fence.

■ Change the verb.
The player yelled across the football field.

■ Drop the "to be" verb.
The crowd focused their attention on the rescuer.

Pronouns

Pronouns in a story can get confusing! Make sure when you use pronouns they are close to their antecedents. A better way to avoid their use in broadcast writing is to use the last name of the person being referenced.

"A grand jury has indicted Mayor Joe Smith on conduct unbecoming of a county official. Smith says he will retain Bo LeBlanc as his defense attorney."

Note that you need to have your facts straight when using solutions 2 and 3. What if an exercise rider raced the horse? Or perhaps the player phoned across the football field.

How do you recognize the "to be" verb? If your sentence contains: **is, am, are, was, were, be, being, or been,** then you have used a "to be" verb.

One simple solution to a "to be" verb involves

dropping the "to be" verb and the "-ing".

He will be following us to the game.

He will follow us to the game.

Do you always want to write in the active voice? No, sometimes the person being acted upon is more important than the person doing the action. You would write, "She was born in 1967"; not "Her mother gave birth to her in 1967." Or, "The candidate was arrested for drunk driving"; not "The police arrested the candidate for drunk driving."

Remember also to write in the present or future tense. It will give your story more immediacy.

Writing Strategies

You will develop your own style of news writing as your career matures, but until then consider using these literary devices. Many of these you'll recognize from your English classes, but never thought of them in the context of writing a news story that will grab viewers' attention.

All the examples used here come from the scripts of Boyd Huppert of KARE-TV in Minneapolis. Boyd has been a featured speaker at venues including the National Writers Workshop, the RTNDA National Convention, the Poynter Institute for Media Studies, and the NPPA Advanced Team Storytelling Workshop. Among his numerous awards are four National Edward R. Murrow Awards, including the Murrow for writing.

Quotations

Never say "quote" in a story, — save that for newspapers. In broadcast we use sound bites — the person actually speaks. If it becomes necessary to use a quote, keep it short, identify the person, pause, then read the quote. Another option would be to create a graphic with the quote and source displayed out of the body of your story, allowing for their use in your story lead in.

Opposing Theme

"On the Lord's day in Granite Falls life along the river went to hell."

"One of the people for whom the stakes are higher, has kept her profile a good deal lower."

Numbers

Never ask viewers to do math in a story. When this happens it draws their attention away from the substance of the story.

When you use numbers, round them up or down.

Example: *The city's budget deficit comes to 13,466 dollars and 68 cents.*

Instead say, *The city's budget deficit comes to more than 13-thousand dollars.* You may use the precise numbers on a graphic.

Write out numbers one through eleven in your copy. *One* instead of *1*, *10-thousand* instead of *10,000*. Using words instead of symbols makes it easier for you or the anchor to read.

Always write out the word *percent* and *dollars*. You may use the terms *nearly, almost,* and *more than/less than*, when rounding. Remember that *over* and *under* refer to placement, not quantity.

Parallel Theme

"For four days they willed the river away from their homes. Now they had mere minutes to leave them."

"Yesterday brought all-day rain. Moving day brought a blizzard."

Analogy

"Don knows numbers like parents know the names of their kids."

"...42 years of teaching broadcast journalism and still hustling like a cub reporter on his way to a car fire."

Metaphor

"The demon at 1030 Morgan is about to be exorcised."

"In a few hours Dr. Hagen hopes to deliver his baby."

Detail

"The only twin towers

in Clintonville, Wisconsin are attached to a dairy barn."

"Four blocks off this Mayberry of a main street...."

Twist a Cliché

"Hastings is at war, but this war is heaven."

"An owner who lost his shirt in the dairy business, but made a silk purse out of a pig."

Positive v. Negative

Writing in a positive is easier to understand than writing in a negative. This is not an issue of good news vs. bad news, but of clarity.

Example: "The mayor says the council members will not be notified until tomorrow."

Better: "The mayor will notify council members tomorrow."

Alliteration

"Ken Staples is persnickety personified."

"The lure for Boyd Hagen is neither nature nor northerns."

Repetition

"All this for town ball, amateur ball, less than minor league ball."

"No one writes carols about this part of Christmas, the waiting in line part, the bored out of your mind part, the part that stands in the way of the merry part."

Supposition

"If we choose our cars for what they say about us, what was Mary Carpenter thinking?"

"If voices could be cast in concrete, these would be monuments to good radio."

Life's Truth

"Few things in Minnesota are as constant as the menu for a Lutheran church supper."

SHELBYVILLE-SHELBY COUNTY
PUBLIC LIBRARY

"Packers and Vikings fans dislike each other so much they can't stand to be apart."

Rule of Threes

"Forget salary arbitration, free agency, and Rolexes."

"Just one metered ramp, one part of snarled freeway system, one shared experience that makes us all Minnesotans."

Life happens in threes: we're born, live, and die; the light is red, yellow, then green; we prepare for a race with ready, set, go. Have you ever heard a "good" country song? Okay, maybe you haven't, but I have it on good authority that every "good" country song has three verses and tells a story. Beginning, middle, end. Don't forget the "Rule of Threes."

Reader

The first and easiest story form is the reader. It is generally short — 15-20 seconds. This is information you've obtained and confirmed. The copy is written for an anchor to read during the newscast. It is a complete story with a beginning a middle and an end, but has no video. See the example at right.

Rewriting

All good writing is rewriting. If you think the first draft of your story is perfect, think again. When you've completed your story read it out loud. If you stumble, perhaps you need to reconsider the sentence structure. If there is no flow, look at your beginning, middle, and end. Did you give a dry recitation of the facts or did you paint word pictures, using words that evoke a feeling? Are there useless words and phrases that seemed appropriate at first, but now cloud the meaning?

You will turn your script in to an executive producer who will go through it suggesting possible changes, proofing for libel, looking for grammatical and spelling errors, checking facts and attribution, making sure it fits the time budgeted for it in the newscast.

A newscast producer will look over your copy and may rewrite your lead-in or tag to include transitional devices.

Finally, an anchor is going to "massage" the copy in the lead-in and tag to fit her speaking style.

Reader Example

Slug: TOMATO CAN	COPY
(ANCHOR) GRAPHIC: TOMATO CAN	(ANCHOR) THE SAYING GOES EVERYTHING OLD IS NEW AGAIN. THE SAME CAN BE SAID FOR THE DEI FRATELLI COMPANY. THEY'VE DECIDED TO REVAMP THEIR CANS OF CRUSHED TOMATOES WITH THE SAME PACKAGING USED DURING WORLD WAR TWO. ALLIED SPIES USED CANS OF DEI FRATELLI CRUSHED TOMATOES TO TRANSPORT MESSAGES OF ENEMY TROOP MOVEMENTS DURING THE WAR. THE COMPANY SAYS THAT A PORTION OF SALES WILL BE DONATED TO HELP VETERANS OF FOREIGN WARS.

The Three A's

I'm big on writing things in threes. The first set of threes you'll learn will start with the letter "A."

Accuracy

Journalists deal in facts. These facts must be sought out and presented to inform our audience. Facts must be accurate; by nature they are truthful. ASSUME NOTH-ING. Facts must be free of judgment. Avoid editorial statements or loaded words in your copy. Accuracy includes correct spelling. A "GFE" — gross factual error — will not be tolerated.

Attribution

All information gathered for a story must be attributed. That means someone must be credited with the facts you gather.

"The families will be moved out because of soil contamination."

Who says they'll be moved out? You? Who says the soil is contaminated? You? I think not!

"Head of the EPA, John Smith, says the families will be moved out because of soil contamination."

Attribution is not an option. You must attribute all of your facts. When writing attribution for broadcast, the attribution/descriptor comes before the name.

Print: Joe Smith, Mayor of Smalltown, was indicted by a grand jury on criminal charges.

Broadcast: A grand jury indicted Smalltown Mayor Joe Smith on criminal charges.

The use of the word "alleged" or "allegedly" is often found when attribution is lacking. Don't be caught! Using these words provide you with NO legal protection.

"Sources tell Eyewitness News…" is not attribution. A source is named. Only on the most rare of occasions would you promise anonymity to a source.

Accountability

The public trusts you to be accountable, that the story you present is accurate. To ensure accuracy, you must hold your sources accountable for the information they give you. This will require you to press the source on the issue to ensure you don't fall prey to an agenda setter.

Things to Avoid in Crime Reporting

When reporting on a crime, you will often obtain initial information from a police report. These reports are often written in police-talk, a form that is not conversational and often confusing.

Words like "perpetrator" or phrases like "in an effort to terminate their use of deadly force" or "the victim received lacerations and contusions to the facial area." No one speaks like that! Perpetrators are the people who commit crimes. They are robbers, burglars, shoplifters, etc. Lacerations and contusions are cuts and bruises.

Suspect

A person is only known as a "suspect" when police can name that person. "The suspect in the murder is the victim's husband."

Otherwise the unknown person is known by his crime. "Police continue to search for the serial killer."

Race

Be careful when using race in a story. The most common error is in its use in a police story. If the police issue a description of a criminal as a "black man, six feet tall, weighing 180 pounds, wearing blue jeans and a t-shirt" ... how many students were just described? Untold! By including race in this case you perpetuate a racist stereotype. Would you have written "white man"? Probably not, you would have said "six feet tall, weighing 180 pounds, wearing blue jeans and a t-shirt." Before you use race, make sure the description is detailed enough to make a difference in finding a person.

Writing Exercise: Active Voice

Change the following passive voice sentences to make them active voice.

1. The coach's point was not missed by the player.

2. The runner was tagged out at first.

3. A verdict has been reached in the murder trial.

4. The medicine has been proved effective in most cases.

5. Houses on the mountain were not threatened by the floods.

6. Police were called to the scene just before noon.

7. The competition is scheduled to begin after the pep rally.

8. The investigation was reopened today.

9. The woman was knocked down and trampled during the parade.

10. He was rejected in his appeals by the Supreme Court.

Writing Exercise:

Pleasantville Bank Robber

Take the following information from the Pleasantville Police and turn it into a 15-20 second reader. Pay close attention to your lead sentence. Your lead for this story can be very creative or very dull. Watch out for information that really has no bearing on the story.

Robbery at First State Bank in Pleasantville at 10 a.m. this morning; man wearing blue jeans, blue jeans jacket, tennis shoes, sunglasses and a ski cap is considered the suspect; didn't show a gun, but the teller says she was handed a note claiming he was armed; after being told to do so, the teller (Miss Amy Lou Scaredstiff) put all her money in a sack and handed it over; he escaped on foot into a residential area north of the bank; acting on a tip, Pleasantville police saw the suspect walking along Rogers Street about an hour after the robbery; he was taken into custody; suspect is identified as Ronnie Roberts, 38, of Smithdale; a sack containing $10,000 was found on him when he was arrested; he is being held on a $50,000 bond following arraignment; no injuries were reported.

Chapter 2

Sources

Where do you get your news? Where do newsrooms get their information? How do reporters get their information?

On any given day you may pick up the newspaper, turn on the TV, or listen to radio to hear the "latest" news. You may also surf the web, pick up a magazine, or talk to your friends. These are all sources of information. I like to use the acronym H.O.R.N. to explain how newsrooms get their information.

H — for HEAR. One of the questions you should ask yourself each day in the morning editorial meeting is, "What are people talking about?" As a journalist you are apt to get wrapped up in the world that is the newsroom. Many times what a newsroom thinks is "important" may have absolutely no appeal to the viewing audience, or it is presented in such a way that the audience doesn't care.

When you go to work in a newsroom more than likely you will be assigned a "beat." A beat is an area that you as a reporter are expected to become an expert in and where you will hear stories. You will develop and contact sources who will share information with you. You must determine whether or not the information is true and newsworthy. Your goal is to obtain this information exclusively before your competitors. Stories you hear about and develop on your on are called enterprise stories.

O — for OBSERVATION. As a reporter you need a keen sense of observation. You need to observe life and people for changes in routine. These observations can lead to enterprise stories. Here are a couple of examples.

Living in one state capital with a striking capitol building, I noticed that the most beautiful view of the building could only be seen in the rearview mirror when I was driving down 3rd Street. Why? Because Third Street was one-way away from the capitol. After our story, Third Street was turned into a two-way street.

Have you ever noticed driving to class in the morning that gasoline prices may be one amount and then when you drive home in the afternoon the price may be 10 cents more? What happened during the day to justify that increase?

R — for READ. If you really want to succeed in this business you must read, read, and then read some more. You need to keep an open mind to other views and ideas. Exposure by reading will help you present a more thoughtful, balanced story. Reading will help you develop story ideas. Make it a habit to daily read the local newspaper, the Associated Press news wire, and to search online news publications and websites.

A word of caution concerning the Internet: just because information is on the web does not make it factual. The web may be a good pool for information, but you must verify that information through other sources.

A good practice is to always have two sources verify information. With two sources you avoid the agenda-setting by a single source. Remember, everyone you interview has an agenda. They want you to tell their story. Now is the time to develop a healthy skeptical attitude. You need to ask "WHY?" a lot, whether it's about a person or an event. You don't want to become a mouthpiece for someone else's agenda. Question authority.

Another word of caution: newspapers, the wire, and other publications also make mistakes. If you repeat as fact information you've taken from a source and do not attribute that source or confirm the "fact," you may be guilty of passing along false information. False information will damage your credibility. If you decide to take basic information from the newspaper, make sure you confirm the information and advance the story to the next level. Duplicating stories from the morning paper for the six o'clock news is lazy reporting.

N — is for NOTIFY. Finally, many organizations or public entities will send information to a newsroom in the form of a news release. These may have some newsworthiness, but often are the agenda of a public relations department.

There is a big difference between the governor's press secretary notifying you of a press conference announcing an increase in state taxes and a press release from a local car dealer about Toyota rolling out a new model. Both have agendas, but which has a greater effect on the viewer? You might turn the Toyota story into one of local economy, using the new model as the hook for the larger story, but a new model alone is hardly a story.

Remember, you must always attribute the source of your information.

Powerful People

Powerful people are often sources of information. Power is intimidating and addictive for both the interviewer and the interviewee, which is why so often those in power are so successful in getting their agenda out. The interviewee is aware of her power. As a young reporter you may find yourself speaking with mayors, police chiefs, politicos, etc. It's easy to be intimidated and these people will use that to their advantage. By scoring an interview with these power-brokers you also have a taste of this power, and may easily fall prey to their agendas. In doing so you may overlook the needed balance for the story. BE CAREFUL.

Finding A Focus

The amount of information you gather can be overwhelming at times. Perhaps it's a very complicated story with numerous interviews, numbers, and historical information. Sometimes it's a spot news story. The chaos and death surrounding a spot news story can be very unnerving. In either case your task is to simplify the information and make it relative to the viewer and listener. Here are some tips on finding a focus:

■ What do you remember? You're the expert, what you don't remember probably isn't worth reporting.

■ What information surprised you the most? The "Gee whiz," "No Way!" "Gotcha" factor.

■ What does your viewer/listener need to know?

■ Can you describe the story in three words? Subject-Verb-Object.

■ What one sound bite essentially describes the story? Will viewers remember it?

■ What picture sticks in your mind?

■ Have you found the 5-W's (Who, What, When, Where, & Why) and a How?
    Remember:
    WHO — is the character, your interview.
    WHAT — is the plot.
    WHEN — is the chronology.
    WHERE — is the place.
    WHY — is the motive.
    HOW — is context.

Writing Exercise: "Louisville Cow"

There is a lot of information here. Read through the information. Answer the questions at the end. Write a 10-20 second reader. Be sure to write in the active voice. Don't forget the 5-W's. Write a clever first sentence. Make sure you find the focus/lead.

A cow that eluded officials for 10 days after it escaped from a meatpacking plant by jumping a 6-foot fence wasn't about to give up its freedom.

Animal-welfare officials shot the 1,100-pound cow with a tranquilizer about 11 p.m. Monday near a corral area that was set up several days ago with a cow brought in to lure the runaway.

Officials were able to tranquilize the cow a second time around midnight. The 7-year-old Charolais cow was loaded onto a stock truck so it could be taken to a farm.

"I weigh 225 pounds, and that cow was dragging me all over the place," said Randall Wright, general manager of the Society for the Prevention of Cruelty to Animals.

The cow will be spared from slaughter because an animal-rights activist and former University of Kentucky graduate Ashley Judd have offered it sanctuary.

The cow escaped from Oscar Meyer Meats on Feb. 15. Louisville police said the animal was captured in the heavily wooded Snow Park where the search had been concentrated from the start.

"This was a free-range cow that is for all intents and purposes a wild animal," police Lt. Burt Kidd said, "This wasn't a cow that was hand fed or milked every day. She only had human contact once a year, and humans were likely to spook her."

The cow's saga got national news exposure and was joked about on the city's broadcast news reports.

Farmers who are accustomed to rounding up wayward

animals were amused by the cow pursuit.

"It's the talk of the town," said Dale Rogers, manger of Hardin County Farm Supply in Elizabethtown, KY.

Rogers said cattlemen he has spoken with were chuckling at Louisville's initial attempts — which included using helicopters and mounted police — to catch the cow. That would have driven the cow into the woods, he said.

■ What is the lead? (No, it's not the first sentence.)

■ What is the "no way"?

■ How would you begin this story creatively?

Additional Writing Exercise

Take the following story and write a :15-:20 reader. It is filled with passive voice and a lot of information that you will NOT need for your story. Don't forget attribution of information in your story. Your job is to take this story and make it broadcast ready.

Arrests in 5-Year-Old Murder Case

Three people were arrested in the slayings of four members of a family five years ago, authorities said.

One of those arrested was already in custody in another case, and two more were arrested Wednesday, Cross County Sheriff Brad Evans said. He declined to identify them.

"No formal charges have been filed at this time," Evans said. "We did extensive interviews (Wednesday) night."

Evan's announcement came on the fifth anniversary of the date authorities believe the Ellis family died — husband Andy, 30: wife Lily, 26: and their children, 6-year-old George and 8-year-old Freda. They lived in the community of Denton, about 23 miles northwest of Pottsville.

The body of Lily Ellis was found the morning of August 30, 2000, on the doorstep of her father's home, where she had apparently made her way after being beaten at her home nearby. Her son was found bludgeoned to death in the Ellis's home.

The family's car was found on a bank of the nearby Elysian Creek. Andy Ellis's body was found in the creek two days later, about a mile downstream from the house, shot in the head.

Freda's remains were not found until two years later, when they were discovered by a hunter.

Then-Sheriff Ron Samples, who went to the Ellis residence after the mother's body was found, said he found the door had been forced open, and the lights and television were on. The boy's body was found on the living room floor.

41

Chapter 3

People, Pictures, Pace

Part of the ingredients of a good TV story can be found in The Three P's: People, Pictures, and Pace.

People — People just love stories about people. People similar to them or people different from them, famous or infamous, downtrodden or powerful people. If you interview someone who has been scammed, injured, or suffered from someone else's action and the viewer has experienced the same thing — in all likelihood the viewer will watch. People are the voices of authority in your stories, they are the voices of compassion, and they are the voices of "every man."

Pictures — Pictures tell a story the way words cannot.

Sometimes the pictures are so "big" they overpower the words. Those are the times when you are better off letting the pictures and the natural sound stand alone, get out of their way. But more often than not, the pictures in a story reinforce the words and vice versa. One of the best habits for you to develop is the act of coming back to the newsroom from a story and logging your videotape. This enables you to write to your video. Remember, the videographer is a photojournalist; you must place the words to enhance the pictures.

Pace — Think of pace as your story's flow, progression. Pace is not the speed at which you read your script; that would be more of an energy level issue. Pace is how you construct your story. How you take different elements of sound and picture and integrate them so as to move the story along. There are different ways to change the pace. Perhaps you begin your package with sound rather than reporter narrative. The sound may be a revealing bite that grabs the viewer's attention or natural sound that sets up the narrative. You might include natural sound breaks that allow the story to breathe. Maybe you butt sound bites together to present opposing views. Think about the placement of your standup. These are but a few ideas on how to change the pace. Just remember that in broadcast, predictability is an opportunity for a viewer/listener to move on. Plan surprises in your stories; think of building tension and then releasing it.

Pictures and Sound

When you write for television there's one more question. Can we get **good video** and **natural sound**? What is television without pictures? Radio! When you write for TV you must employ all the previous writing criteria, and you must also write to your video.

How often have you watched a story on the local news

and watched video totally unconnected to the written words? Too often I'm afraid. When you see video that seemingly has nothing to do with a story, you're watching **wallpaper video**. It's video just there, out of context. You must give the video context. Video should support your words and your words must support your video. If you say "frog," you must see a frog. Maybe in your mind you know why the video is being used, but unless you make that clear to your viewer, they'd have to be mind readers fixated on you!

Never expect someone to recognize video from the past as relevant to the story you're doing today. Take the time to explain why that video is important enough to be with your story. Also when using "file" / "morgue" video (video from a previous story) make sure you also graphically indicate that it is file by inserting a date over the video or the word "update"

The other part of the equation is sound. There are two types. **Primary sound**, which is your reporter track and interviews, and **natural sound**, which is that ambient sound that takes place while you are gathering your video for TV or information for radio. This ambient sound will be added when you're editing your story to help engage the viewer/listener. The best example I can think to give you is a sports story. Have you ever seen game highlights where the video is all action, but you don't hear the cheers of the crowd, the bounce of the ball, the contact hit? Just silence? Now you understand why natural sound is important. Natural sound is also a pacing device, a break from your words to establish a resonance with the viewer/listener. Natural sound can be found at the beginning, middle, and end of a story.

Interviewing

Your primary sound and information will be found through interviews. Before you rush out the door, consider this:

■ **Determine the purpose of the interview.**

Are you conducting the interview for primary information or background information?

■ **Research the topic and the person**

Go in knowing as much about the topic as possible. Do not trust the interviewee to educate you or you will only get their version of "The Truth." Ask yourself these questions:

▲ Does the person have the information I need?

▲ Is the person available for interview?

▲ Will the person provide me with the information I need?

▲ Can the person freely and accurately transmit the information to me?

▲ Is there anyone else on staff who may have had dealings with person and can offer guidance?

Make sure you have all the information available to you before you go into an interview. Know the answer to as many of your questions before you ask them. Watch out for and recognize smoke screens and attempts to take you off track.

Asking Questions

It's easy to say, "Make a list of your questions." But it is better to know what your options are in asking questions so you can ensure you get the answers you'll need for your story. There are many types of questions:

Open-ended questions
Broad questions, often specifying only the topic.
Highly open-ended: Tell me about yourself. What is life like in Lexington?
Moderately open-ended: Tell me about your first job.

Closed-ended questions
Limited answer options; specific response required.
Highly closed-ended: What is your class standing?
Bipolar: Do you like or dislike the new Macs?
Moderately closed-ended: How old are you?

Primary questions
Introduce topics or new areas within a topic.
Describe your ideal job.
How do others describe the gardens you design?

Secondary questions
Attempt to elicit more fully the information asked for in primary questions.

Leading questions (avoid these)
Imply or state an expected answer in the question.
"Don't you think the U-2 tickets are too expensive?"

Loaded questions (avoid these)
Imply both an answer and some negative belief.
"Do you still beat your wife?"

Ask for Subjective sound ~v~ Objective sound

You always remember what you feel more than what you know.

For example: I remember coming upon the scene of a horrible accident on my day off. There were three vehicles involved and bodies scattered everywhere. Two small trucks carrying teenagers in the back had been drag racing. They came upon a curve and both swerved trying to miss an oncoming car. I called the station and waited for the videographer to arrive. The information officer for the police department arrived later and we began our interview.

Objective: "Can you tell me how many vehicles and victims were involved in the accident?" "There were two small pickup trucks. The blue one had a driver and two passengers all in the cab — two more in the back. The black one had a driver and a passenger in the cab — two more in the back. The driver and passengers from the blue truck were killed when they struck a tree - the occupants in the back were thrown out and killed. The driver in the black truck has been transported along with his passenger — the occupants in the back were thrown out and killed. The white sedan had only the driver who has been transported. We won't be releasing names until next of kin have been notified."

Objective: "Was alcohol involved?" "At this time we can not say. We'll wait for blood tests before making that determination, although several open containers were found in the trucks and around the accident scene.

Subjective: "What was the first thing you thought when you arrived on the scene?" (The officer took a deep, ragged breath.) "In 15 years on the force, I've never seen anything like this. It breaks my heart and I know there are going to be heartbroken parents out there tonight."

The power was in the subjective sound bite. The other questions gathered information needed for the story, but the officer's reaction is what the audience remembered.

Interviewing Tips

Here are some tips based on ideas from the pros at the Investigative Reporters and Editors organization. You can find them online at www.ire.org.

■ **Ask for help.** Asking for help doesn't mean you don't know. People like to be asked for help. Asking them to help you understand will leave them feeling in control. Maybe you're a little confused and lost, and you need help figuring things out. In helping you, people just may tell you what they know.

■ **Be prepared.** You need to know what you're talking about. Study the subject - and the terminology - so you don't fall victim to agenda setting. Know your questions and what the answers could be.

■ **Listen.** You shouldn't be trying to tell people what you know. You want to get what they know. Some of the best questions are "Why?" "How?" "What do you mean?" "I don't understand" and "Can you give me an example?"

■ **Talk to everyone.** Think outside the box. Figure out everyone who might know something. Talk to them all. Don't be afraid of returning to a source for clarification. Getting stories is like assembling a jigsaw puzzle without knowing how many pieces there are or what it might look like.

■ **See people face to face.** You can't look a telephone in the eye. And if you're in someone's office or living room, they can't hang up or put you on hold or ask you to call back another time — when they won't be in. Get moving instead of waiting on call backs!

■ **Challenge your sources.** Don't let them spoonfeed you their version and accept it. Say you don't understand; say it

More Interviewing Tips

■ Arrive early.
■ Have a list of prepared questions. There is nothing wrong with having a list. Remember the intimidation factor.
■ Dress appropriately.
■ Pay attention to your camera setup. Do not shoot in front of a window.
■ Check your microphone levels.
■ Eliminate any extraneous noises.
■ Make small talk while setting up. This helps put the interviewee at ease.

During the Interview

■ Meet the interviewee's eyes.
■ Make sure the interviewee speaks to you, not the camera lens.
■ Watch your body language. Watch their body language for cues.
■ Ask open-ended questions.
■ Do not rush to the next question. Listen to the response as it may require a follow-up question. Remember you have a back-up list of questions.
■ Silence works to your advantage. Don't be afraid of it.

doesn't make sense from what you know from other people. Ask them "How can you be certain?" Let them prove it to you — with more details, other names, any documents.

■ **Never trust your source, at least not completely.** Double-check — that's another reason to talk to everyone so you corroborate the "facts."

Silence does not reflect on your ability as a reporter. Often if there is a verbal lull, an interviewee may feel the need to fill it with additional information — information you may not have gotten if you had rattled on to the next question.

After the Interview

■ Stay seated and keep your mouth shut while your photographer shoots cut-aways.
■ Look at the interviewee.
■ Do not nod your head. If your photographer uses a cut-away of you nodding your head you appear to be in agreement with your interviewee. Remember journalism shows no bias.

■ **You set the rules.** If the interview is background or not-for-attribution, make certain you and source have the same definition of how the information will be used. Most of them want to tell you something anyway and will do so, at least on a background basis that allows you to pursue confirmation elsewhere. Don't accept a source's "I changed my mind" after an interview.

■ **Respect the gatekeepers.** She may only look like a secretary, but if you want to get past that desk, be nice! Bringing her coffee or a treat can't hurt. She can also be a source for other stories in the building as she probably knows all "the dirt" going on in other offices and departments.

The Truth

A few tips on sorting out what is truth:

■ **Never Assume.** Check everything. Always doubt. Most journalism errors occur from careless oversight rather than malice.

■ **People will tell you what they only think they know.** Sources may tell you what they suspect, think, speculate, or have heard from others, without really knowing. A handy test to use: Ask your source, "How do you know that?"

■ **Use your common sense.** People may, with honest intent, tell you different versions of the same event. Look for what makes good, simple, common sense. One warning: a story that sounds too good to be true often is just that — not true.

■ **People rarely tell 100% lies.** Most people are not capable of fabricating total falsehood. They may change, color, exaggerate, omit, selectively use, misstate or misunderstand certain facts. Their tale will be woven around some pieces of truth. You must strip away the layers to find what is true.

■ **Look for what is missing.** At any stage of a story it may be helpful to draw up a checklist of what you do not know. Develop a sense for what doesn't quite add up.

■ **Don't rush the truth.** Yes you must meet deadlines, but a deadline is never an excuse for misinformation and the loss of your credibility.

■ **Run scared.** Worry about what you may not know, what you may have missed. If you are a reporter who is worried about being wrong, you have a much better chance of getting the story right.

These guidelines were written by James Polk, NBC News with the advice and assistance of David Hayes, Kansas City Times, Prof. Carl Stepp, U. of Maryland, and Prof. Steve Weinberg, U. of Missouri and reprinted with permission of Investigative Reporters and Editors.

Ten Questions Every Good Reporter Needs to Ask

■ How is this supposed to work? It's important to know how the system works. Say you are covering an air emissions story; do you know how the air is cleaned after leaving the factory? If not, how will you explain to the audience? How will you recognize an error?

■ What is or isn't counted? Can I count it? Remember on the second question that "yes" or "no" can mean a story. What if you wanted to know how many students lived in the dorms and when you went to residence life they couldn't tell you. The negative answer is a bigger story than the positive answer.

■ Where did you get that? Where did the information originate? It's important to go all the way back — get it straight from the horse's mouth — no hearsay allowed in the courtroom or journalism.

■ Who else would know that? This is especially important in corroborating facts, plus it gives you another source that may give more or different information.

■ Am I at the beginning of the story? What would have had to happen to get the answer to my question? Have I asked that? These are more than questions of origin; they are questions you need to ask yourself before you go on your interview. Your report must have context, you must know that background or you leave yourself open to error.

■ Can I have a copy? Now, not later! Don't be afraid to request documentation, it is the backbone of good journalism. If your interviewee refers to a document ask for your own copy; again it's a context/fact issue. Don't wait until you're back at your desk. Understand that what you're after may only be a part of a much larger document and there are times that you will have to pay for such documentation. Also be aware that your interviewee may crawfish on you later or even go so far as to change the documentation (yes, it happens!)

■ What would "they" tell me? When covering an issue it never hurts to ask one side what the "other" side might say when asked the same question. Just remember to give the "other" side the same opportunity to respond concerning the opposition. You are the beneficiary of having both agendas and can better prepare follow-up questions.

■ What do "you" think? Pick out a trusted friend to review your copy, someone who will shoot straight with you, and tell you what, if anything you are missing.

■ What does all this mean? What's the big picture? If you can't answer these questions for yourself — think how your viewer/listener must feel! Too often reporters take a myopic view on a story. It's the lack of follow through that makes a news consumer crazy.

■ What else are you working on? Never leave a source, especially a source on your beat without asking this question. Part of your job and ultimate goal is to provide enterprise reporting that your competition will not have. Asking this simple question of an interviewee will alert you to upcoming events that you can preview in a story. It's the difference between proactive and reactive reporting.

Sound bite or SOT or bite

This is simply an interview. You may be sent out to interview someone on a topic or perhaps to a press conference and the producer may only want a SOT from your endeavor. You will write an anchor lead into the sound bite indicating where the sound should start, select the sound bite's in and outs, write out the sound bite verbatim, and follow the sound bite with an anchor tag. Beginning, middle, and end.

Writing into SOTs

Whether you are writing SOTs, VO/SOTs, or packages, you must introduce the speaker before they speak. This can be a bit tricky. You must be careful not to "parrot" the sound bite.

For example:

"Joe Smith said there was nothing he could do to save the drowning youngster, 'He got caught up in the rip tide and there was nothing we could do.'"

Better:

"Joe Smith watched helplessly from the pier, 'He got caught up in the rip tide and there was nothing we could do.'"

Writing into a SOT is part of the attribution process. Remember that in broadcast the speaker's title/descriptor goes before his or her name:

Mayor Wanda Smith

Sheriff Roy Canard

Professor Scoobie Ryan

Community advocate Jaime Pittenger

Voice over/sound bite or vo/sot or vob

When there is compelling video to help tell your story along with your interview, a producer may ask for a

VO/SOT or VOB. You will provide the anchor with a lead-in, you will indicate where the VO should begin in the copy, where the SOT should go, and then include an anchor tag to be read after the SOT.

Voice over or VO (TV)

You may be sent on a story that will have no sound or interviews. You must write to the video, giving the facts, and setting it in a format in which the anchor will read a sentence or two before the video begins followed by your copy matching the video. The anchor reads over the video — not you.

Anchor Lead-ins

Every story begins with an anchor lead-in. Reporters write lead-ins, producers tweak them for flow, and anchors read them. A good anchor lead-in tugs on the viewers' interest, attracting them to the story. You have only seconds to make sure the viewer/listener sticks with you and doesn't pick up the remote. Too often reporters will wait and write the lead-in after they've written the package. In a hurry to get back and help the videographer edit, the reporter may write as their lead-in the same first two sentences of the package. It is a good habit to start writing the lead-in first, then the package, followed by the anchor tag.

A package lead-in usually consists of two sentences. First a teaser type sentence, followed by a reporter attribution sentence for a package. When writing a VO or VO/SOT the teaser sentence read by the anchor will stand alone without reporter attribution. Below are the two most common types of lead-ins.

Question lead-in
"Looking for a little extra cash at the end of the month?

Kelsey Kirkpatrick says it's easier to get than you might think."

Statement lead-in

"It's not every day you meet a man walking around with 10-thousand dollars in a paper bag. Mahalia Webb introduces us to Garrick Reed — a real life bag man."

Notice how neither lead-in gives away the story. Many times there is a tendency to put too much information in the anchor lead-in. Keep it simple. Broadcast is about simplicity. Stay away from "So & So has the story" — how boring! Placing the reporter's name at the beginning of the second sentence helps eliminate dull and uninformative lead-ins.

Anchor Tag

A tag is the logical conclusion to a package, a VO/SOT, or sot. A tag is written by the reporter and read on the set by the anchor. It includes additional information to bring the story full circle.

More often than not, you'll have more information than you can possibly place in a story. Make it a habit to save a tidbit of worthwhile information for the tag.

Phone numbers and website addresses make poor tags. If you must use this information for a tag make sure you prompt the audience to grab a pen and paper to copy the information. Make sure you present the information on a graphic.

"Now if you'd like more information about the kindergarten roundup grab a pen and paper we've got a phone number and web address for you (graphic) The Fayette County Kindergarten Roundup. Call ###-#### or pre-register on the web at www-dot-####.edu. We'll give that address again later in the newscast." Or you may point the audience to your website where the information can be posted.

Inclusive Voice

When you write for broadcast you write in an inclusive voice rather than an exclusive voice.

"Eyewitness news has learned...." Not "Governor Edwards told me...."

Remember you're writing in a conversational manner. You don't want to seem aloof. Your viewers choose to let you into their home each evening. Make them glad they chose your station.

SOT Example

Slug: TRAVELING TOMATO CAN	COPY
(ANCHOR) GRAPHIC: TOMATO CAN	(ANCHOR) FOR MOST PEOPLE, A FREE TRIP AROUND THE WORLD WOULD BE A ONCE IN A LIFETIME EXPERIENCE. AS WORLD TRAVELER SONNY DEI FRATELLI TELLS US, TOO BAD THIS CAN OF TOMA-TOES COULD NOT ENJOY THE RIDE.
(TAKE SOT) (CG:Sonny Dei Fratelli/ World Traveler) (LENGTH : 15) (out cue: "… UPS to track it for me")	(TAKE SOT) "I was on vacation in Italy and I saw the can at a local market, which shares our last name. So I thought my daughter, who is studying abroad in Japan, would get a kick out of it, so I sent it to her. When she never received it, I was puzzled, so I called U-P-S to track it for me."
(ANCHOR TAG)	(ANCHOR TAG) U-P-S TRACKED THE CAN DOWN TO TAIWAN, AFTER IT HAD ALREADY STOPPED IN 44 OTHER COUNTRIES. AFTER A FULL YEAR OF GLOBETROTTING, THE CAN FINALLY MADE IT TO JAPAN.

VO-SOT Example

Slug: TOMATO CAN CASH	COPY
(ANCHOR) GRAPHIC: CAN BRAWL	(ANCHOR) A BRAWL IN THE GROCERY STORE AISLES, THAT'S WHAT SOME SHOPPERS FOUND AT THE KROGER AT BEAUMONT CENTER
(TAKE VO) (CG:Kroger/ Beaumont Center)	(TAKE VO) STORE EMPLOYEES DEALT WITH SCRATCHING MOMS, SHOUTING DADS, AND BROKE COLLEGE STUDENTS, ALL TRYING TO GRAB THE LAST CAN OF DEI FRATELLI TOMATOES. THE DEI FRATELLI COMPANY RELEASED DETAILS OF A PROMOTION INVOLVING A CAN STUFFED WITH CASH INSTEAD OF TOMATOES. CHRIS SMITH GRABBED THE LAST CAN IN LEXINGTON.
(WIPE TO SOT) (CG:Chris Smith/ Injured Shopper) (LENGTH :10) (Out cue: "…that's all that matters.") (ANCHOR TAG)	(WIPE TO SOT) "I don't mind the bump. I got what I came for, that's all that matters." (ANCHOR TAG) WHEN THE DUST SETTLED THE LUCKY CAN HOLDER WAS GRACE ALEXANDER WHO SAYS SHE'LL PROBABLY SPEND THE MONEY ON THIS MONTH'S BILLS.

VO Example

Slug: TOMATO CAN	COPY
(ANCHOR) (TAKE VO) (CG: Letta Tomato Processing Plant/ Elizabethtown) (ANCHOR TAG)	(ANCHOR) A SHORTAGE OF CRUSHED TOMATOES? (TAKE VO) THAT'S THE WORD FROM THE LETTA TOMATO PRO-CESSING PLANT IN ELIZA-BETHTOWN. ABOUT TWO-THIRDS OF THEIR PRIZE WINNING TOMATOES HAVE BEEN DESTROYED BY THE OVER USE OF A PESTICIDE. MANAGER OF OPERATIONS, LARRY JONES SAID THAT THE FAMOUS DEI FRATELLI TOMATOES WOULD NOT BE AVAILABLE IN STORES FOR THE NEXT EIGHT WEEKS. THE TOMATOES ORIGINAT-ED IN 1927 AND ARE PROCESSED USING ONLY TOMATOES FROM ELIZA-BETHTOWN. (ANCHOR TAG) THE COMPANY HAS HIRED A PESTICIDE SPECIALIST TO CONDUCT AN INVESTIGA-TION.

Writing Exercise: VO/SOT

Read through the following story. At the end you will find a list of video shots. You must write to your video and write into your sot. A good rule of thumb in deciding how much video you'll need is to write a sentence, then place the video. Press "return" and write the next sentence and place the video. Remember, one thought per sentence, one theme per story.

"Georgia Storm Disrupts Air Travel"

Hundreds of travelers who thought they were just passing through Hartfield International Airport in Atlanta were forced to spend the night on cots after storms canceled dozens of flights.

By late Friday, 368 arrivals and departures at Hartfield had been canceled, according to Georgia Department of Aviation spokesperson Bonnie Monet. Hartfield handles about 2,400 flights daily.

Flights into and out of the airport were delayed as much as two hours as thunderstorms passed over northern Georgia, knocking out airport radar equipment and power to thousands of area residents.

A backup radar system took over until repairs were made to the main system.

Adam Jones of Fly Us Airlines said Friday's storm was the worst of the summer. Wind gusts of up to 50 miles per hour and sudden changes in wind direction forced the airline to cancel 246 arrivals and departures at Hartsfield.

The storm made worse an already miserable summer for air travel out of Hartsfield, largely because of Fly Us Airlines's impasse on a new contract with its pilots union. The airline has canceled more than 23,000 flights since April due to pilots who refused to work overtime. Fly Us and the pilots agreed on a new contract last month.

At the peak of the storm, which the National Weather

Service said dumped nearly three inches of rain, about 53,000 customers of Georgia Electric lost power. About 300 crews worked overnight to restore power, said Mike Justice, a spokesperson for the utility.

Video available:
Wide Shot-Hartfield airport
Medium Shot-Parked planes
Close Up-plane
ws-ticket desk
ms-agent & passenger
cu-hands typing on keyboard
ws-tower
ms-control room
cu-radar screen
ms-arrival/depart screen
cu-"canceled"
ws-waiting area
ms-passengers
cu-kids playing
sot- Bonnie Monet/Atlanta Dept. Aviation
"Of the 24-hundred flights we handle each day, we were forced to cancel 368."
You will need to write to the available video above.

Writing Exercise: VO (TV)

Take the video from the Georgia Storm and write a :20 voice over. Be sure to write to your video

Chapter 4

Package

A package is the backbone of a newscast. You will be expected to turn at least one package per day, if not more. A package is a story complete with an anchor lead-in that you will write to introduce the story; copy that you will write and read telling the story, interviews, stand-ups, and an anchor tag that you will write to end the story.

Remember every story having a beginning, middle, and end? Here the anchor lead-in is the beginning. The package is the middle, and the anchor tag is the end.

Now within the package — your story — there is also a beginning, middle, and end. You set up the premise, you have the facts, and you go full circle with the conclusion.

Stand-up

After you've completed all your interviews, you will need to shoot a stand-up. A stand-up is video and sound of the reporter on tape that is inserted into the package.

Stand-ups fulfill a couple of needs in a story. Stand-ups can be used to create empathy with the viewer, to take the viewer to the scene, to serve as a transitional device or bridge from one location to another, from one point of view to another. Sometimes stand-ups can be used to present information for which you may have no video. Stand-ups can also be used to illustrate an abstract idea.

You may end a package with a stand-up, you may have a stand-up in the middle (a "bridge"), but never begin with a stand-up. If the most important information of the story is the reporter on camera speaking, perhaps the story needs a new approach.

Verbatim

When writing a package you must include the verbatim of sound bites and stand-ups in your story. Your producer or executive producer will be responsible for approving the content of your story and the verbatim will be necessary in fact checking and checking for legal liabilities. Most news operations also provide closed captioning for the hearing impaired audience. Your written words and sound bites appear at the bottom third of the screen for those viewers to read. So yes, that means you must write every single word.

Standard Out ~v~ Non-Standard Out

Another package element is the reporter out. A standard out is the closing a reporter uses at the end of a package. The reporter will give his/her name, possibly his/her location, and who they're reporting for; "In Scott County, I'm Tiffany Hunter for Action News" or "I'm Max Mitchell for

Action News."

A non-standard out is one without a reporter closing. There is only the last sentence of your package, which you will provide to the newscast director, so he'll know your story is over. A non-standard out most often will occur if you are doing a "live" wrap around or a set piece.

Do not confuse a reporter out with an anchor tag. A reporter out is part of a package. An anchor tag follows the package.

Stand-up ~v~ Live Reporter Wrap

A term you'll hear producers use is "change the trick." When it's obvious that you and your competition will all have the same lead story, producers (and reporters) start looking for ways to make their story standout from the rest. One of the easiest ways to do this is to send the reporter out to be "live" for a reporter wrap around.

Do not confuse a "live" wrap around with beginning a package with a standup.

In a "live" wrap, the anchor on set tosses to the reporter who is in the field. With a wrap you will write the anchor toss in addition to a lead-in that you will read before your package. At the end of your package you will have a "non-standard" out — you will tag your own package and toss back to the anchor in the studio.

A word of caution here: if you know you are doing a "live" wrap remember that you cannot end your package with a standup. Think about it, you're standing there in your package, then you're standing there in your live shot!

The following is a completed script for a live reporter wrap. Pay close attention to anchor and reporter exchanges going into the package and following the package. When you write a "live" wrap, you are responsible for writing and setting up this exchange.

Writing Process

You've received your assignment and are out the door. Your interview went off without a hitch and you've gathered your video.

Back at the station you need to log your videotape, making note of specific video you want to write to in your script, which sound bites you'll use, and which standup.

Focus on your lead. The lead is the aspect of the story that's most important. It should be the compelling reasons to watch/hear this particular story. The reason the audience cares about the story.

Remember to have a beginning, a middle, and an end; to paint word pictures; to tell a story.

After you've written your anchor lead-in, package, and anchor tag, read your script aloud. Watch for words that might trip you up, non-conversational language, and awkward phrasing.

Let another reporter read your script. The old saying of not "seeing the forest for the trees" applies to reporters. Sometimes you may be too close to the story and with your knowledge of the facts you may overlook an important aspect that makes the story easier to understand. If there's a question statement or fact, call the source back for clarification or more information. Better to be a little embarrassed and get the facts right, than to allow pride to compromise your story and your credibility.

When you're finished you must get your script approved by the executive producer or the show producer.

Start editing. Deadlines are your constant companion in broadcast.

Reporter Wrap Example

(ALI)	(Ali) A GALIANO POLICE OFFICER IS ON ADMINISTRATIVE LEAVE TONIGHT AS STATE POLICE INVESTIGATE A CLAIM OF SEXUAL MISCONDUCT FILED AGAINST HIM.
(TAKE DOUBLE BOX)	(take double box) STEVE ALLEN JOINS US LIVE WITH THE STORY.
(STEVE)	(STEVE) ALI, THE WOMAN CLAIMS THE INCIDENT HAPPENED LAST FRIDAY MORNING AS SHE WAS GETTING READY FOR WORK. THE POLICE OFFICER SAYS IT NEVER HAPPENED AND IS CONFUSED BY THE ALLEGATIONS
(take package) (cg: "Jane")	(take package) "I FEEL ALL OF MY RIGHTS HAVE BEEN TOTALLY TAKEN AWAY FROM ME. ALL OF MY DIGNITY. ALL OF MY PRIDE, ALL OF MY SELF WORTH HAS BEEN ROBBED." WE'LL CALL HER JANE. JANE SAYS LAST WEEK. A GONZALES POLICE OFFICER WHO MOONLIGHTS AS AN APARTMENT SECURITY OFFICER. USED HIS PASS KEY TO GET INTO HER APARTMENT AND RAPED HER.

	"I WAS GRABBED FROM BEHIND MY NECK. I BEGAN TO SCREAM NO. NOT TO DO THIS. MY MOUTH WAS COVERED AND PUSHED TO THE FLOOR. THE REST OF MY TANK TOP WAS TAKEN OFF, AND I WAS HAND-CUFFED IN FRONT OF ME. EVERY-THING WAS FORCED FROM BEHIND."
	JANE SAYS ONE OF THE CUFFS LEFT A BRUISE.SHE SAYS SHE WENT TO THE HOSPITAL, AND POLICE WERE NOTIFIED. STATE POLICE SAY THERE IS AN ACTIVE INVESTIGATION, BUT NO CHARGES YET.
(cg: Lt. Mark Edwards/ State Police)	("WE'RE GOING TO MAKE SURE THE T'S ARE CROSSED AND THE I'S DOTTED AND MAKE SURE THIS THING IS COMPLETED BEFORE WE RUSH ANY TYPE OF JUDGEMENT IN THIS CASE."
	THE MAN IN QUESTION IS Isaac Massey. A 20-PLUS YEAR VETERAN OF THE GALIANO POLICE FORCE. MASSEY ADMITS HE HAS A PASS KEY, BUT EMPHATICALLY DENIES THE RAPE.
(cg: Isaac Massey/ Galliano Police)	"IF I HAD ANY GUILT WHATSO-EVER, I WOULDN'T BE TALKING

TO YOU, IN FACT I MIGHT GET IN TROUBLE FOR TALKING TO YOU NOW, BUT I'M INNOCENT, I HAVE NOTHING TO BE GUILTY ABOUT."

MASSEY AND JANE HAVE CONFLICTING STORIES.BUT BOTH AGREE ON ONE THING.THEY WERE NEIGHBORS AND CASUAL FRIENDS.

" I WOULD LIKE TO KNOW WHY? BECAUSE I'VE BENT OVER BACKWARDS TO HELP THIS LADY"

(STEVE)	(Steve) GALIANO POLICE CHIEF BOB LAWSON IS OUT OF TOWN, BUT ISSUED THIS PRESS RELEASE. IT SAYS ADMINISTRATIVE LEAVE WITH PAY IS STANDARD PROCEDURE WITH AN INVESTIGATION INVOLVING A POLICE OFFICER.
(take double box)	(take double box) ALI. AGAIN WE WANT TO POINT OUT THAT OFFICER MASSEY HAS **NOT** BEEN CHARGED. THE STATE POLICE INVESTIGATION CONTINUES TOMORROW WITH A POLYGRAPH TEST ON OFFICER MASSEY.
(ALI)	(Ali) THANKS, STEVE

Package Example

Slug: HOT TOMATOES	COPY
(ANCHOR) GRAPHIC; TOMATO	[ANCHOR] IF IT'S HOT IN L-A, THEN IT'S ONLY A MATTER OF TIME UNTIL THE NATION PICKS UP THE CRAZE. ERIKA SIMPSON TELLS US ABOUT THE LATEST FAD MOVING EAST.
(TAKE PACKAGE)	[TAKE PACKAGE] TOMATOES… THEY'RE RED, ROUND, AND JUICY. BUT NOT EVERY TOMATO CAN MAKE A CLAIM TO HOLLY-WOOD FAME. BIRTHED FROM THE "CHEAPEST TOMATOES IN MONTANA" THIS CAN OF CRUSHED TOMATOES WENT FROM RAGS TO RICHES WHEN ACTRESS CATHERINE ZETA JONES ASKED SPECIFI-CALLY FOR THE BRAND - DEI FRATELLI.
(CG: Catherine Zeta Jones) (LENGTH :10)	"These tomatoes are "Prima Quality" they contain no added salt or fat grams. I won't eat anything else on my spaghetti." THAT STATEMENT CAUSED

	A RUSH AT LOCAL FOOD OUTLETS LEAVING SHELVES EMPTY AND SUPPLIERS LIKE MARK SMITH WITH TOMATO ON THEIR FACE.
(CG: Mark Smith/ ProFood Suppliers) (LENGTH :10)	"We've called the processor in Montana and had six cargo containers shipped Federal Express, just to meet yesterday's demand."
(STANDUP) (CG: Erika Smith/ Reporting)	Although they wear a fancy brand name, Montana growers say these tomatoes originally sold for fourteen cents a pound. The going current price, 2-50 a pound. In Hollywood, I'm Erika Simpson, Action News.
(ANCHOR TAG)	[ANCHOR TAG] GROCERY WAREHOUSE SUPPLIERS REPORT A 50 PERCENT INCREASE IN THE DEMAND FOR DEI FRATELLI TOMATOES IN JUST THE PAST WEEK.

Writing Exercise: Train Derailed

Take the following information and write a package. Indicate the video you would use in your package. Sound bites have already been selected for your story, but you must place them. You will also write a standup and place it in your package.

With a billowing cloud of fuming sulfuric acid hovering over her neighborhood, Lisa Brown knew it was time to get her four children out of the area.

The family, along with their pet Chihuahua, was among 42 people sleeping on cots Sunday night at Broussard High School after a train carrying 10,600 gallons of the hazardous chemical derailed in the Middletown community near Loxville.

No one was injured, but at least 3,000 people were evacuated. Brown's husband John stayed behind.

"I kept calling my husband, trying to get him to come up here, and he said 'If I'm going to go, I'm going to go,'" she said. "My main concern was the kids."

"I told my husband, 'If you're going to be stubborn, stay here. But I have to make sure these kids get safety.'"

Two of three locomotives and the first 24 cars of a 141-car "mixed freight" train left the track at about 11:30 a.m. EDT, said Susan Schmidt, spokeswoman for Virginia-based Norfolk Southern railways, which owns the train and track.

The train — which also was carrying freight including bricks, aluminum, limestone and two military vehicles — was traveling from Loxville to Birmingham, Ala., when the accident occurred, she said. The cause remains under investigation.

The highly corrosive acid, used in manufacturing, was transported as a liquid, but became a gas upon release. Fumes continued to escape from the wreckage on Monday morning.

Emergency crews on the scene were being hindered by heavy fog rolling off nearby Port Smith Lake. Alex Jones of the Lox County Emergency Management Agency said workers were having trouble distinguishing the smoky white acid vapors from the fog.

Lox County Sheriff Bill Henry said it would be at least Monday night — and possibly Tuesday — before residents will be able to return home.

"It is just a slow, tedious process," he said. "There's a lot of liquid down there. It is fuming and it is very dangerous. We are all just going to have to bear with it."

Emergency workers were notified of the accident by a woman living near the tracks. She called 911 after hearing noises from the derailment, officials said.

Twenty people and one emergency worker complained of minor skin and lung irritation and were taken to a hospital, where they were treated and released, said Sgt. Jim Dempsey, a member of the Loxville Special Hazards Team.

Norfolk Southern sent two teams to assist with the evacuation and cleanup. Crews from several states also responded with specialists, Henry said.

In Washington, Tammy Wilson, a spokesperson for the National Transportation Safety Board, said the agency has dispatched a team to investigate.

Video Available:

SOT: Lisa Brown/Evacuee
"I told my husband, 'If you're going to be stubborn, stay here. But I have to make sure these kids get to safety.'"
SOT: Bill Henry/ Lox County Sheriff
"It is just a slow, tedious process. There's a lot of liquid down there. It is fuming and it is very dangerous."
WS: Officer diverting traffic
CU: Officer directing traffic
WS: Derailed train cars

MS: Derailed train cars
CU: Derailed train cars
MS: Haz Mat crews working scene
CU: Haz Mat worker
MS: Empty Houses
MS: White chemical cloud about train cars
CU: White chemical cloud leaking from train car
WS: People going into shelter
MS: People inside on cots
CU: Child playing with dog in shelter
Cu: Train car with hazardous chemical warning
MS: Workers spraying foam
CU: Foam on train cars
Standup: You write it and place it!

Writing Exercise:
Package with Live Wrap

Take this story and turn it into a "live" reporter wrap around a package. You pick the SOT's you want to use. Place the video as you would edit it. Remember you're reporting live, several hours after the accident for the early morning show.

Two Killed in Texas Bus Attack

A passenger slashed the throat of a Greyhound bus driver as the bus traveled down a Texas freeway, causing it to career out of control, authorities said. Two people died and dozens were injured.

The bus, heading from Austin to Houston, flipped on its side Monday evening and slid into a cotton field about 500 feet off Interstate 35, officials said. The bus was carrying 49 passengers.

Officials said the attack was not related to terrorism.

According to witness accounts, the man rose from his seat, walked briskly up to the driver and attacked him before 9 p.m., said Lt. Mike Sanchez of the Hays County Sheriff's Department.

"The driver was actually cut in the neck," Sanchez said. "He struggled, tried to defend himself and lost control of the bus.

Authorities caught the suspect as he tried to run away. His name was not immediately released, and he was arrested on suspicion of assault with a deadly weapon, Sanchez said.

"I saw a dude walk fast and pull past to the front (of the bus)," said passenger Stanley Brown, who suffered only minor injuries and later was reunited at a community center with his wife. "I'm feeling blessed."

Twenty-seven people were taken to hospitals, including

three in serious condition, officials said. The others were still being evaluated, but most appeared to be in stable condition, nursing supervisors said.

Other passengers received minor scrapes and bruises.

Authorities originally stated that the driver was one of the two who died, but the Hays County Sheriff's Department later said that he survived. He was in serious condition.

There was no word on what the motive might have been, but Sanchez said it did not appear to be anything that would require federal involvement in the investigation.

Janice Bradford, a spokeswoman for Greyhound Lines, said a hot line had been set up for friends and family members of passengers to call for information.

"Our top priority right now is taking care of all of the passengers as well as the driver and their families," Bradford said.

Almost exactly a year ago, a passenger on a Greyhound bus in Missouri cut the driver's throat, causing a crash that killed seven.

Dallas-based Greyhound, the nation's largest bus service with 20,000 departures, has hired a private company to screen some passengers with electric wands but has inspectors at only a portion of its terminals.

Video & Sound for Bus Accident Package

WS-emergency vehicles
MS-EMT loading injured person
MS-EMT working on injured person
CU-EMT face
CU-EMT hands
MS-victim on stretcher
CU-victim holding bandage to head
WS-more injured being carried to emergency vehicle
CU-2 law enforcement officials talking into radio

MS-victims huddled on side of road
MS-victim being treated in emergency vehicle
CU-IV bag hanging above victim in emergency vehicle
MS-EMT talking with victim
MS- sheriff deputy walking through debris
WS-bus on its side
MS-Greyhound logo
MS-hospital ER entrance
INTW-Lt. Mike Sanchez/Fresno County Sheriff's Ofc.
INTW-Stanley Brown/Passenger
INTW-Janice Bradford/Greyhound Lines

Chapter 5

Videography

Whether you call it "film," "pictures," or "video," the old adage, "A picture is worth a thousand words" holds true. In our earlier discussion we talked about pictures defining television. As a TV journalist you must think not only in terms of factual information, but also in how pictures will portray or reinforce your words.

Many of you grew up with a video camera in your home. It was a fairly simple piece of technology and was passed from person to person to capture family moments. You probably held the camera, pushed the button, and recorded indiscriminate "scenes" that may have been viewed once and never again. It may have told your family's story, but didn't translate to those outside your family. You must now become a videographer or photojournalist, which means others will see your work. Crafting a story through video takes foresight and planning.

Quality video doesn't just happen. If your pictures don't relate to the story, they are nothing more than wallpaper. What is it that you notice when you walk into a room that's wallpapered? More often than not, nothing. Is that the type of impression you want your story to leave? Or maybe the wallpaper is awful (picture here your mother's huge floral print that has been up as long as you can remember). You don't want extremes; you want the pictures and the words to do a handshake.

Video Sequencing

Finding a focus as a photojournalist is much more than discriminating between a clear or blurry frame of video. Just as you must find the focus of your story before you write, you must also find the focus before you shoot. If you are a "one-man-band," which means you are the reporter, videographer, and editor all rolled into one, you will quickly learn how important it is to be focused in your writing and your shooting. The end result is easily edited and tells a complete story. You will understand better the video needed for the story you're going to write and how to gather the pictures, and where to put them in your copy. And since you are this "one-man-band" you know that the entire burden for the story and meeting all the deadlines falls squarely on you. This kind of responsibility will work to your advantage as your career advances. When you are teamed with a photojournalist you will find the importance of conveying your focus so that once back at the station, your writing and pictures meld.

When you begin to shoot you will want to shoot in a video sequence. A video sequence is comprised of a wide, medium, and tight shot. Using sequencing helps transition the video by varying the focal length of the shots.

The sequence may take a very minimalist approach such as this:

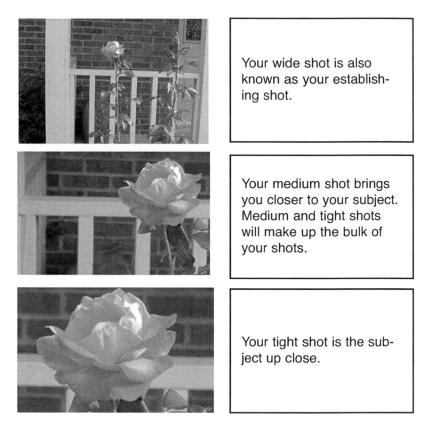

Your wide shot is also known as your establishing shot.

Your medium shot brings you closer to your subject. Medium and tight shots will make up the bulk of your shots.

Your tight shot is the subject up close.

By using video sequencing you will also be able to perform match edits. Match edits are video shots edited so that the action within the frame at one perspective or focal length matches the video in a following shot at a different perspective or focal length. For example: perhaps you are shooting at a construction site and a bulldozer is moving dirt. Your wide shot would show the bulldozer moving in a direction pushing dirt. Your medium shot will show the blade pushing the dirt in the same direction. You might have a second medium shot of the operator — still moving in the same direction. Then your tight shot could be of the operator's face, or the pile of dirt and the blade. The most important thing about match edits is that the video looks as though you had multiple cameras and you were switching between them. All action must match. By using match edits your video will have a much broader shot selection adding interest to your story. When shooting for match edits, you will have to shoot the repetition of the action from different focal lengths while focusing on different aspects of the action.

The most common mistake among beginning videographers is the tendency to shoot nothing but wide shots. All wide shots edited together result in very boring (wallpaper) video.

Here is another example of a sequence. Perhaps you're doing a story on a new drug, but you have no manufacturing video from the pharmaceutical company. You could use your sequence this way:

"XYZ Company has introduced a new drug that doctors hope will bring big changes in the treatment of cancer."

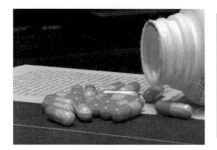

"The drug called 'Zapit' works to increase the number of antibodies that directly attack the cancer cells."

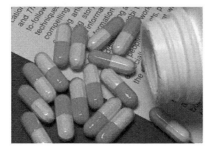

"With newly completed testing in a local hospital, XYZ expects to gain FDA approval by the first of next year."

Just by taking a bottle of the medication and building a very simplistic sequence you can cover :10 - :12 in your package. You would also want to shoot the bottle with the label.

Camera Parts

Before you begin the technical aspects of the camera, let's make sure you understand some of the terminology.

The **viewfinder** is the one-inch by one-inch black and white electronic screen you will find on the left side of your camera. Just like your TV at home, this screen has a brightness control and a contrast control. Learn to set the brightness and contrast by using the color bars generated inside the viewfinder. Doing this before you shoot will save you agonizing doubt as to whether or not you have enough light for your video.

The **servo** sits to the right of your lens. It fits in the palm of your right hand, if you have the camera on your shoulder. There is a strap your hand fits into to secure your grip. Your forefinger and middle finger will rest on the rocker bar, which makes your lens zoom in and zoom out. Your thumb will be on the rear of the servo where a start/stop button will control your video recording. The start/stop button is marked **VTR**.

The **lens** protrudes from the front of the camera body. At the end of the lens you will find a sunshade, a somewhat flexible ring that sits on the end of the lens. This provides protection from the sunlight hitting directly in the lens, causing a flare. It also is the easiest part of the lens to grab and focus.

Focusing

When you are ready to shoot look, through the viewfinder to locate the object/person you want to capture on tape.

Zoom all the way in on the object, so that it fills the majority of your viewfinder. Focus by turning the lens' focus ring or lens shade. When shooting an interview, focus on the person's eyes. When you've got the shot focused, zoom out and frame to a wide, medium, or tight focal length.

If you have trouble focusing there are a few things to check:

■ Are you too close to the subject? If so, back off a couple of feet, zoom in and refocus.

■ If your lens has a macro adjustment for extreme close-ups, try using it.

■ If physical distance is not the problem, the back focus of your camera could be out. Learn how to make this adjustment to your lens.

If none of these ideas work, frame and focus the best you can, without zooming in.

Perspective

Learn to change your perspective. That's more than zooming in or out and changing the focal length of your lens. Use some "in your face" techniques. Shoot from above. Shoot from below. If you're doing a story on safety-proofing your house for the new baby, get down on the floor and see life from the infant's perspective. Life doesn't happen from a five-foot-tall point of view. Give us point of view shots.

Hold That Shot

Once you've pressed "record," count 10-15 seconds at each focal length while you hold the camera very still. If there is the slightest camera movement, start counting over. Your average edited shot will only last perhaps five seconds, but you never know when you might need more to cover your reporter copy. Note: camera movement does not mean subject movement within the frame. Movement **within** the frame always makes for more interesting video. You may have to hold your shot a little longer so you can match your edits, but object movement is a good thing; camera movement is not.

Pans, Zooms, Tilts

Pan (camera movement from side to side), zoom (lens movement in or out), and tilt (camera movement up or down) may be the mainstay of MTV and reality TV, but they are less important in TV news. Remember this, all movement must serve one of these purposes: to reveal, to draw attention to, to transition. As you watch the different news programming, pay attention to how often you see these movements used. When a movement is used, the movement must come to a complete stop before the next edit can take place.

Camera Set-up

After securing the camera to the tripod, add the battery or power supply. If you're shooting a lengthy event, you may want to use an AC adapter rather than batteries. Batteries are referred to as "bricks."

Turn the camera "on" and insert your field tape. A field tape is a blank tape you'll record your images on. NEVER insert the tape and then turn the power on. This almost always results in a jammed tape.

Light Temperature

Light temperature or

Color temperature is a very important aspect of shooting and achieving the correct color balance for your video. You must start thinking of light as a temperature to select the correct filter for your shooting circumstances and to properly white balance. **White balancing is the process of correcting the color for the light temperature.** Any time the light temperature changes you should white balance regardless of the fact that your filter may not have changed. For example: if you are shooting inside with fluorescent light you will white balance for that temperature on a clear filter. You may go to another room where the light is a mixture of daylight and table lamp, you will have to white balance for that light temperature. Then you may enter a third room where the light is again fluorescent, but from a very high ceiling; this requires a third white balance. All of this is done on one single filter.

It is not enough to have the correct filter — you must make allowances for the light temperature to achieve the correct color. Video with an incorrect white balance will be blue or orange.

White Balancing

Now you're ready to select your filter and white balance the camera. To white balance, select something white — a piece of paper does great — and make sure it is reflecting your current light temperature. Zoom all the way in so as to fill the viewfinder with white. Locate the white balance button or toggle switch and activate it. Inside your viewfinder you should see a shift in the video indicating a change. Some camera models will say inside the viewfinder "white balance ok."

Filters

Many cameras have a standard three-filter system:

Filter #1 is a clear filter. It lets in as much light as possible. The actual temperature for filter #1 is 3200K. You would use filter #1 when shooting inside or at night.

Filter #2 has a dichroic aspect to it. Daylight filters blue. With filter #2 you will be able to shoot outside on an overcast or cloudy day and have the white balance correct for true color. The temperature for filter #2 is 5600K.

Filter #3 (5600K+ND) has a neutral density coating. Filter #3 permits you to shoot outside in the bright sunlight.

Regardless of which filter you use, always remember you must white balance with every change of the lighting.

Low Light Situations

There will be times when you need to shoot video under low light conditions. You can address this problem by adding additional light through the use of a light kit or a battery-powered sun gun. There also are times you can't. One way to adjust for the low light is to boost the video gain. Most professional cameras have the capability to boost the video levels by +9 db and +18db. If you are shooting at night, your video level to +9 or

"M." If you still can't get a white balance, take it a step further and go to +18 or "H." Boosting the video level will add graininess to your video, much like enlarging a photo. Avoid it when you can, but use it as you need to.

Audio

Check your microphones and make sure they are working properly. To do this you must use headphones or an earpiece. Always do a level check before pressing the record button. There is no excuse for coming back with an interview and no sound.

Audio on channel 1 should be your primary audio, such as interviews and stand-ups. Make sure you use a lavaliere or hand microphone for interviews and stand-ups. You want a directional microphone plugged into channel 1.

Audio on channel 2 is natural sound. This microphone is omni-directional and usually attached to the front of the camera. You never want to use this as an interview microphone since it will pick up any ambient sound in the vicinity of your shoot.

If you are shooting an interview and there is noticeable ambient sound such as a heating/cooling system, radio, etc., do what you can to eliminate the excess noise. Turning off such devices for the short time of an interview is not an unreasonable request.

Another approach would be to turn off the nat sound mic during an interview so that it doesn't compete with your directional microphone.

Meters

Remember to check your record level meters. If the volume on your headphones is turned up you may not notice that the audio is recording below the optimum level. Just because it sounds good on your headphones doesn't mean it will sound good in the edit booth.

Tripod Usage

Because we want to eliminate as much movement as possible, you must use a tripod. Gonzo photojournalism and cinema verite' may be the rage, but the serious videographer still relies on his/her "sticks" for every shot. Nothing is more distracting that the constant frame movement associated with hand held cameras.

There are a couple of tricks should you get stuck somewhere without your tripod:

■ Get as close to the subject as you can. Zoom in, focus, and then pull all the way out.

■ Brace yourself. Think of using your arms and elbows as a tripod on a tabletop.

■ Lean against a solid object such as a wall or a tree to steady yourself.

■ Brace the camera. Use a flat steady object to shoot from.

■ Hold your breath while recording.

Framing Your Interview

When you are ready to videotape your interview, set the tripod and the camera up so that they are head-on and at eye level to your interviewee. When framing your interview, remember you want the interviewee's eyes one-third of the way down from the top of the screen, leaving two-thirds of the screen below the eyes. This allows room for super information (see p. 92).

Your shot should be a basic head and shoulders shot. You should have some headroom — or empty space — above the interviewee's head when you look into the viewfinder. You don't want to have too much headroom or your interview will look like a hostage tape, but you don't want to cut off the top of the person's head by being framing too tight. The bottom of your viewfinder should cut across the interviewee's chest just above the breast.

During the interview, the person being interviewed should look at the reporter, not at the camera.

When an interview is shot extremely close, a la *60 Minutes*, it has an effect on the viewer. It may leave the viewers feeling uncomfortable — and that may be the purpose. Or it may leave the viewers feeling that they have "the truth" from staring the interviewee in the eyes and watching him blink.

Interview Obstacles

Once you get to an interview there are a few things you want to watch out for when setting up your camera.

First, pay attention to the background behind your interviewee. You don't want anything "growing" out of their head. The viewers will be too busy laughing to hear what's being said.

Second, make sure the interviewee isn't sitting in front of an exposed window. If you can't close the curtains or shades, ask the interviewee to move. Otherwise your interview will be backlit. Backlighting occurs when the light source behind the person is stronger than the light source striking the person's face. The result is the automatic iris in the camera, which reacts just like the iris in your eye, shuts down and becomes smaller, letting in less light. Less light means the face of the person being shot will be dark.

Third, if you cannot shoot the interviewee head-on, remember to lead her. If she is at an angle and you center your shot, it will appear as if she's talking into the "wall" of one side of the screen, and there will be excess empty space on the other side. Lead her by placing the empty space in front of her face, not behind her head. Never shoot a straight profile shot.

Jump Cuts

There will come a time when you want to manipulate an interviewee's sound bite. Sound bites should be short, but sometimes a person may begin one thought, jump to another, then return to the original. Taking the middle out is simple enough. That's called a "butt bite." The problem with a butt bite is that you are left with the same subject, at the same focal length, but without continuous action. The subject of the video appears to jump from one location on the screen to another. This is called a "jump cut."

Cutaways

To avoid jump cuts, you will always shoot cutaways when you shoot an interview. You can shoot cutaways either before or after an interview. Think of the cutaway as the tape that will hold the two sound bites together and hide the seam.

A cutaway can consist of a number of different shots:

■ You can shoot a two-shot (the interviewee and the reporter) from behind the reporter and over their shoulder.

■ You can shoot a two-shot from behind the interviewee and over her shoulder.

■ You can shoot a medium or tight shot of the reporter alone. This is called a "reverse." You may shoot a tight shot of the reporter making notes in a notebook or the interviewee's hands. Any of this video may be used to cover the jump cut of a butt bite. This would be a video-only edit since the audio of the continuous thought is your goal.

■ Another cutaway option would be to shoot video of what the interviewee is referring to and use that video to cover part of the sound bite that is not continuous.

The 180-Degree Rule

When you are shooting cutaways, you must observe the 180-degree rule. Draw an imaginary line through the center of the reporter across to the interviewee. This imaginary line extends to infinity. Now set your camera up either to the right or the left side of the reporter. For example, perhaps you choose the right side. When you have finished the interview and begin to shoot your cutaways you will always stay on the reporter's right or the interviewee's left. Do not cross the imaginary line.

Supers

Leave the dramatic, extreme close-ups to *60 Minutes*. There should be enough framed video below the chin to insert a super. A super, lower third, or CG (character generator) is typed information that is superimposed over the video and is used most often to identify a person, a location, or a date. Supers often have two lines of information that take up the lower third of the screen. The top line will be someone's name; the second line or sub-super will be information that better identifies the person. For example: Teresa Isaac/Lexington Mayor, Lee Todd/ UK President. Some names, such as the president, the pope, and well-known celebrities, require no sub-super. It takes most people at least three seconds to read a super. It will take the director one second to insert the super and one second to remove the super. All in all a sound bite should be at least five seconds long for a "clean" super. If shorter than five seconds, do not super. If you use more than one sound bite with a person you only have to super them once.

Cutting Audio

When you are ready to edit the first thing you have to do is record your audio. After you've had your copy approved:

■ Mark your script for emphasis and breathing before you go to the audio room.

■ Always wear your headphones.

■ Stand while you deliver your copy.

■ Wet your lips.

■ If you "pop" your P's and hiss on your S's, turn the microphone sideways and speak past the screen.

■ Your delivery tone should match your story tone (upbeat, somber etc.) It should always be in an authoritative manner at a "performance" level.

If you are recording your audio onto blank videotape, once you've pressed "record" there is no need to stop recording until you are finished. You do not read/record the anchor lead-in or tag or your soundbites/interviews, but record all other reporter copy you have written. It's best to use a countdown before/between each version.

For example you might say: *"Cut 1, Take 5, 3, 2, 1..."* That would indicate you're on the first cut of reporter copy, your fifth attempt and the standard 3,2,1 before you speak. If the fifth take is the one you like, pause and write that on your script. Such notations and countdowns will be big helps as you rush to edit.

Editing

Now it's time to start editing. Just as you've shot in sequence, you'll benefit from editing in sequence. You want to vary your shots not only in subject, but also in focal

SHELBYVILLE-SHELBY COUNTY
PUBLIC LIBRARY

length. You will need to alternate between medium and tight shots when you butt them together. You'll also want to be aware of mixing inside/outside shots and day/night shots.

If you go from outside to inside, use a standup to transition or bridge the location change. If you go from nighttime to daytime make sure you reference it in your script.

For example: The fire lit up the night sky, burning for hours as firefighters worked to bring it under control. In the light of day residents picked through the ashen remains of the historic boarding house."

One of the first questions you'll have when editing your first story is, "How long should the shot last?" There is no rule on this one — the best thing to do is make edits at natural breaks in your audio phrasing or when the script calls for a specific video change. Most shots should last at least three seconds unless you're doing quick edits for effect.

Remember that viewers have a very short attention span. You want to put your best pictures and sound right away in your story. Grab them while you can!

Index

Other journalism titles from Marion Street Press, Inc.

The Book on Writing
The Ultimate Guide to Writing Well
By Paula LaRocque

Paula LaRocque's new book is the culmination of over three decades of writing, editing and educating. Read *The Book on Writing* once and you'll be a better writer. Read it several times and you'll be among the best. $18.95

Championship Writing
50 Ways to Improve Your Writing
By Paula LaRocque

Journalists everywhere love Paula LaRocque's gentle way of teaching better writing. This book is a collection of her best columns on journalistic writing from Quill magazine. $18.95

Heads You Win
An Easy Guide to Better Headline and Caption Writing
By Paul LaRocque

Heads You Win explains the process of writing headlines and captions, from developing the ideas to making the text fit. $12.95

The Concise Guide to Copy Editing
Preparing Written Work for Readers
By Paul LaRocque

The Concise Guide to Copy Editing walks the reader through the copy editing process. Topics include rewriting leads, pruning copy, fixing quotations and many other sticky copy editing situations. $12.95

Understanding Financial Statements
A Journalist's Guide
By Jay Taparia, CFA

Understanding Financial Statements demystifies P&Ls, balance sheets and other essential documents, and tells journalists how to uncover the goods. $24.95

Math Tools for Journalists - 2nd Edition
By Kathleen Woodruff Wickham

Math Tools for Journalists explains math concepts in layman's language and shows how these concepts apply to situations journalists face every day. $16.95

Order at www.marionstreetpress.com